THE ART OF MICRO & SMALL CAP INVESTMENT

- BUILDING A MULTI-BAGGER PORTFOLIO

CA BHASKAR ABHISHEK

"Keep your dreams alive. Understand to achieve anything requires faith and belief in yourself, vision, hard work, determination, and dedication. Remember all things are possible for those who believe.-"

Gail Devers (American athlete)

I had always dreamt of writing a book. Tried multiple times. But failed to finalise a book. However, with consistent efforts and strong will, I could finish this book and also my dream of writing a book. With this first book of mine, it would be the beginning of my career as an author and I hope to spread my knowledge and experience to everyone who gets a chance to read this book.

Being a Chartered Accountant and investment enthusiast, I aspire to write more such books on investment and personal finance and this is just the beginning. This book may not be attractive to those who have already built their career in investment, but it will serve the purpose of those who want to learn value investing or multi-bagger investing from scratch and in layman's terms.

Although this is a basic book that guides micro-cap and small-cap investment, my readers can expect an advanced version for small-cap and mid-cap portfolio building soon in the coming years.

Since this book is a dream come true for me, I would love to dedicate this first book of mine to *'Myself'*.

Hope you love it

Contents

Acknowledgements

"Because true belonging only happens when we present our authentic, imperfect selves to the world, our sense of belonging can never be greater than our level of self-acceptance."

- Brené Brown (American academic and podcaster)

Since this book is completely out of my thoughts and experience, I would be the best person to acknowledge myself.

Of course, it is said that - Phenomenons don't happen unless they are destined to. So, I would love to acknowledge my destiny, this universe and the entire ecosystem that supported me while writing this book and kept me motivated.

Finally, I am thankful to all the beautiful people in my life who helped me reach this stage of life where I have learned enough to share my knowledge with the world.

My learning is ongoing and I have miles to go. I hope to share more of my learnings through a few more books that I might write in future.

Till then happy reading and enjoy learning. !!

About The Author

Dear Readers

I introduce myself as Bhaskar Abhishek from Patna, the Capital City of Bihar. I am an Engineer turned Chartered Accountant. I was first introduced to the Stock Market in February 2010 as my first demat account was then opened. Who did it at such an early age for me ? That's a different story and I shall discuss about that in my other book.

Since then I have been through the financial statements of multiple companies and gained an understanding of how companies' stock prices behave after any event. I started my part-time stock market career as a trader until I understood the power of long-term small-cap investment. Since November 2013, when I started my Journey in CA Curriculum, I have been through thousands of Balance Sheets and Profit and Loss Accounts.

After completing my CA, I joined PwC SDC as an Audit and Assurance Associate wherein I had multiple opportunities to read the Financials of Business Giants of the world. Those times also skilled me fair enough to analyse the financials for investment purposes.

am often asked for stock suggestions by my friends, colleagues or family members for long-term holding. However, I believe that one should not rely on some tips and recommendations, rather if possible get a fair understanding. For a person belonging to a non-commerce background, it will take time to become a pro in such investments. But yes, it can be done. So, why not start learning a bit?

So, finally, I decided to document all my experience and understanding in the form of a book that could help a novice to self-learn the art of multi-bagger investment. And here I present my book,

" The Art of Micro & Small Cap Investment" - building a multi-bagger portfolio

Hope you like it !
Regards
CA Bhaskar Abhishek

ABOUT THE AUTHOR

About The Book

Hey Investing Minds !!

You are here because you are someone who belongs to my mindset about investing. Thanking for purchasing this book. And now, let's explore this book together.

This book is like a dream come true for me. I always aspired to write a book on investment and finally, I did it. Whenever it is the first time someone, you put your heart and soul into it and so did I.

This book is purely based on my practical experience with micro-cap and small-cap investment. It has been written considering a child in my mind who has just stepped out of his/her 12th grade and wants to learn investment. It will also serve the purpose of teaching someone who is in his 50s and is reluctant towards new learnings. So, I have tried to keep it as simple as possible.

I would urge my readers not to invest in the stocks mentioned in the book blindly. Those stocks are not rccommendations from my side. Those happened to be a part of my portfolio. So anyone investing directly in those stocks without doing their research and incurring losses will not be my responsibility. Please read the book thoroughly and make your notes and only then try doing some investments with a small amount as discussed in Chapter 1 'Warning'.

Benjamin Graham (an American financial analyst and investor) once said - ***"In the short run, the market is a voting machine, but in the long run, it is a weighing machine."***

"Someone is sitting in the shade of a tree today because someone planted a tree a long time ago."- Warren Buffet

(an American businessman, investor, and philanthropist who currently serves as the chairman and CEO of Berkshire Hathaway)

As I said in my introduction, I also used to be a trader until I learnt the power of investment. Investment is always the best choice for wealth creation as compared to trading which serves as the purpose for generating income.

Investing will make you financially independent, not trading.

Do you want to be financially independent ?

Yes ! So, what are you waiting for ? Start turning the pages and build your fortune. This book is waiting for you to explore it.

Happy Investing !

Please leave me your feedback on my LinkedIn profile below. Waiting to hear from you soon.

Regards

CA Bhaskar Abhishek

The author can be contacted on Linkedin @ **https://www.linkedin.com/in/ca-bhaskar-abhishek/**

My Investment Style is the product of my thought process and my risk appetite. Please don't copy it.

- CA Bhaskar Abhishek

CHAPTER ONE

WARNING

> *"An investment in knowledge pays the best interest." — Benjamin Franklin (Founding Father of the United States)*

Investment in micro-cap and small-cap stocks are very risky. Since this book is to educate you on micro-cap and small-cap stock investment, you might get excited about investing as soon as possible. But hold, you could lose all your money because of the following reasons :

1. Stock might get delisted
2. You may lose patience and sell your stocks at a loss.
3. You might not be able to identify the potential stock and become a victim of compromised stocks.

Good News!

These can be handled. How ?

Being a learner, you should practice such investments with the minimum possible amounts. For example, if you identify a potential stock, try not to invest more than what you can afford to lose. I started my journey with Rs 1,000 per stock because that was what I could afford to lose.

"Why only Rs 1000 ?"

Micro-cap stocks are highly risky in nature as they have the potential to wipe off your entire capital. Hence precaution is of utmost importance. Mind it, I am not talking about due diligence, I am talking about precaution. Due diligence means doing proper research before making any investment. But precaution is something else. Let's understand.

You must have heard the quote, **"Never put all the eggs in the same basket"**

This quote is the backbone of Multi-bagger or Micro-cap investment. It means you cannot think of investing your money in one single micro-cap stock. For me, it has to be a minimum of 10 stocks. So as a beginner in micro-cap investment, when I started, my initial capital was **Rs 10,000 (1000 * 10)** which I could afford to lose.

"How it works ?"

Micro-cap investment is not done for 20% or 30% return. It is invested for a minimum 3X-5X return and if the research is well done with the spices of patience, it could go up to 1000X.

So, let's suppose 4 out of 10 stocks fail to retain their capital. But 6 of them grew by 2X. What's the impact?

- Invested Capital : 1000*10 = 10,000
- Lost Capital : 1,000*4 = 4000 (it will not be entirely lost, there will be some salvage value)
- Grown-up capital : 1000*6*2= 12,000

- Let the stocks grow for 3X
- Grown-up capital : 1000*6*3= 18,000

Similarly, you can wait for the entire portfolio to grow up to 5X or 10X according to your research on stock potential to grow more and holding period. The learning curve will improve with time and patience and obviously more practice.

Crux

Be cautious while investing as a beginner. Invest only that amount that you can afford to lose. Initially, the purpose of investment should not be profit-making, rather it should be learning and sustainability.

> *"Important Warning*
>
> *This book contains a discussion about small-cap and micro-cap stocks from my portfolio. Readers are not encouraged to invest in those stocks without doing their own research or due diligence. Any loss incurred out of such investment will not be the author's responsibility. So maintain your calm, think multiple times, do your research and invest wisely because this is your hard-earned money, not mine."*

Thank you

CHAPTER TWO

WHY MICRO-CAP OR SMALL-CAP ?

""I make no attempt to forecast the market—my efforts are devoted to finding undervalued securities."- Warren Buffett"

""Thousands of experts study overbought indicators, head-and-shoulder patterns, put-call ratios, the Fed's policy on money supply...and they can't predict markets with any useful consistency, any more than the gizzard squeezers could tell the Roman emperors when the Huns would attack." -Peter Lynch (American investor)"

Market Capitalization or Market Cap in simple words is the product of the total number of outstanding shares and market price of any company. Let's understand Market Capitalization first with the help of a few examples.

- **Rashtriya Chemicals and Fertilizers Ltd (NSE: RCF)**

Total Number of Shares Outstanding - 55.17 cr
Market Prices (Closing as on 10.09.24) - Rs 186.98
Market Cap as on 10.09.24 - Rs 10,315.69 cr

- **Godfrey Phillips India Ltd (NSE: GODFRYPHLP)**

  Total Number of Shares Outstanding - 5.20 cr
  Market Prices (Closing as on 10.09.24) - Rs 6,844.2
  Market Cap as on 10.09.24 - Rs 35,589.84 cr

- **Electrosteel Castings Ltd (NSE: ELECTCAST)**

  Total Number of Shares Outstanding - 61.82 cr
  Market Prices (Closing as on 10.09.24) - Rs 221.56
  Market Cap as on 10.09.24 - Rs 13,696.84 cr

By now you must have understood what Market Capitalization is. Also, there is a hidden learning in the illustration. Can you guess?

It's easy. Market Cap of a Company keeps on changing every moment with the change in its share price. Accordingly, based on the market capitalisation, companies are divided into 4 broad categories.

1. Micro Cap - Market cap upto 500 cr
2. Small Cap - Market cap from 500 cr to 5,000 cr
3. Mid Cap - Market cap from 5,000 cr to 20,000 cr
4. Large Cap - Market cap above 20,000 cr

Therefore, with a drastic change in the Market Price of a Stock, it shifts itself from one category of market cap to another. It may be a positive shift or a negative shift.

Hence Micro Cap Stocks not necessarily mean those stocks which are in early stage of their business. Micro

Cap segment may also have distressed companies i.e. those companies that once used to be Small Cap, Mid Cap or Large Cap, but do to some reason lost majority of their market price per share. Few examples are :

1. Yes Bank Ltd
2. PC Jeweller Ltd
3. Jet Airways (India) Ltd

Can you think of more? If not, try finding out a few for yourself.

Why Micro Cap Stocks ?

Companies with low market capitalisation have hidden opportunities, especially those with strong fundamentals. It means such companies may build a fortune if they work on their full potential with optimum utilization of the resources. How ?

The easiest example today is "**Ola**"

Ola took off with the concept of being an aggregator for public transport like taxis and autos. Slowly it expanded its operation to Ola bikes and then Parcel, Insurance, Ola Scooty and so on. And this may only be the beginning for Ola and it may have miles to cover. As the company expands its business, its value will keep on increasing and gradually it will be a multi-bagger one day if managed properly with strong fundamentals.

Other examples are "**Zomato**", "**Oyo**" and so on.

Therefore micro-cap stocks with strong fundamentals are potential multi-baggers with up to 100X return. But wait !! Don't be so excited.

Great return always carries Greater Risk!

There is always a risk that these micro-cap companies can face their decline phase if mismanaged. *Hence micro-cap investment must be made only when the fundamentals are very strong and the prospects of the company are promising. If not, please don't invest.*

Activity:

Let's screen 10 stocks for a multi-bagger portfolio

- Using any screener, get a list of stocks having market cap less than and up to 500 cr
- Out of these stocks filter out those having market prices less than Rs 500. (For multi-baggers, I normally prefer low-priced stocks. However, it is not necessary that micro-cap stocks can't have higher prices. With experience, if you are comfortable with high-priced stocks, it is ok to go with them.)
- Separate the list into two categories. *Category 1*: Distressed Stocks (i.e. having high prices in the past but have lost their market cap due to some mishappenings). *Category 2*: Normal Stocks (i.e. stocks that have been growing normally and nothing severe has happened in the past that could erode their market cap)

CHAPTER THREE

STOCK HUNT - WITH OBSERVATION

"Everything that happens happens as it should, and if you observe carefully, you will find this to be so. -Marcus Aurelius (Former Roman emperor)"

"To acquire knowledge, one must study; but to acquire wisdom, one must observe. - Marilyn vos Savant (American columnist)"

Have you ever thought about which of your day-to-day consumption commodities or services are listed ?

Although I have been in stock investment since February 2010, I realised the power of visualisation in December 2022, when I was stuck in a traffic jam due to a heavy crane from ACE (*Action Construction Equipment*). Although the jam was irritating for me, looking constantly at the ACE Crane, I just thought to google its company name which turned out to be Action Construction Equipment Ltd and to my surprise, it was a listed small-cap company.

I researched a bit more about its fundamentals and found it a potential buy. I bought the stocks at around Rs 300 per share in December 2022 and sold it at around Rs 900 per share in January 2024. Below is the screenshot of my transactions for your reference

Transaction History **Stock Code: ACTCON**

Add Transaction

Edit	Action	Quantity	Transaction Price	Brokerage inclusive all taxes	Transaction Charges	StampDuty	Segment	STT Paid / Not Paid	Remarks	Transaction Date (DD/MM/YYYY)	Exchange
	Buy	●	326.2	8.68	0.02	0.00	Rolling	Paid	icicidirect	13/12/2022	NSE
	Buy	●	308.7	2.73	0.01	0.00	Rolling	Paid	icicidirect	02/01/2023	NSE
	Buy	●	308.7	2.73	0.01	0.09	Rolling	Paid	icicidirect	02/01/2023	NSE
	Sell	●	911.06	3.79	0.15	0.00	Rolling	Paid	icicidirect	20/01/2024	NSE

Splitted Records(system modified)   Bonus Records(system added)   Unmatched sell transactions where no buy transaction has been identified prior to the sale date

* STT is NA for Gold ETF

Amazing !! Money got 3X in just 1 year

Was it that easy for me ?

No !

The observation was just an idea for a stock. After I learned about this stock, I had to research whether the stock was worth investing in extensively. We shall learn about the financial parameters that I used in other chapters.

"Note: We have so many products daily to consume from listed companies. Definitely, that will give you an idea. But what we are looking for is a micro-cap or small-cap company with strong fundamentals and fewer competitors "

Another example from my portfolio where I used observation for investment - ***Olectra Greentech Limited***

Post-COVID is the era of green energy. The entire world is moving towards sustainable energy and green energy is one of the most suitable options. In the past 3-4 years we have seen drastic growth in the sustainable energy sector, especially the e-vehicles. Not only scooters, cars and e-rikshaws, we have also come up with e-buses that are used for public transport.

Now, it is a matter of critical thinking that manufacturers of cars, scooters and e-rikshaws can grow in number as there will be an increase in demand. But where e-buses are concerned, it is likely to have low competition in this sector. So whenever I encountered an e-bus, I was able to find it from Olectra Greentech.

Then what ?

I went ahead to research it's fundamentals and found it a promising buy and below was the result.

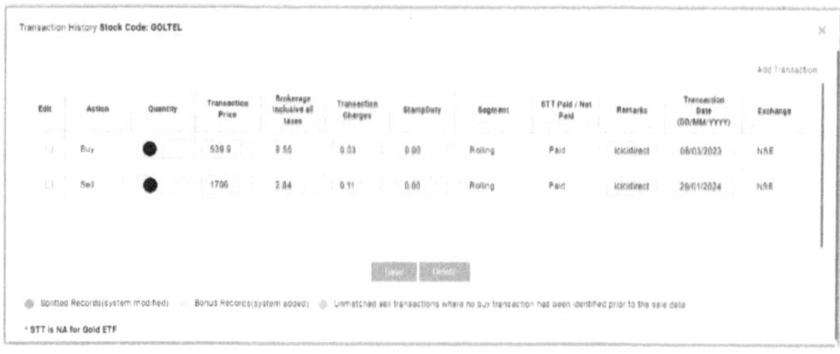

Transaction History **Stock Code: GOLTEL**

Add Transaction

Edit	Action	Quantity	Transaction Price	Brokerage Inclusive all taxes	Transaction Charges	StampDuty	Segment	STT Paid / Not Paid	Remarks	Transaction Date (DD/MM/YYYY)	Exchange
	Buy	●	539.9	8.56	0.03	0.00	Rolling	Paid	icicidirect	08/03/2023	NSE
	Sell	●	1706	2.84	0.11	0.00	Rolling	Paid	icicidirect	29/01/2024	NSE

◉ Splitted Records(system modified)   Bonus Records(system added)   ◉ Unmatched sell transactions where no buy transaction has been identified prior to the sale date

* STT is NA for Gold ETF

Amazing !! It became 3X in just less than 1 year

I bought it @ Rs 540 in March 2023 and sold @ Rs 1,706 in January 2024. My investment got trippled in just 9 months.

Again the same question. Was it that easy for me ?

No !

Finding the stock name was just an idea. Next, I had to research the stock fundamentals to identify its potential for growth.

Similarly, there are more such stocks in my portfolio that gave 2X to 5X in just 1 year. The idea is not to show growth.

The idea of this chapter is to make you understand that you are not required to go mining the stock list to find a micro-cap or small-cap stock for a potential multi-bagger. You just need to keep your eyes open and get an idea of a stock. Once you find a stock then do the research for its investment potential.

"*Key Takewayay*

God has given us a pair of beautiful eyes. Please utilize it wisely because not everyone has the privilege of having those beautiful pairs. If you are blessed with those, use them to build your fortune."

Activity:

Find and list down 10 stocks based on your surrounding observation having a market capitalization of less than 5,000 crores. Also, make a note of the sector to which the company belongs and its market capitalization.

1. ______________________________
2. ______________________________
3. ______________________________
4. ______________________________
5. ______________________________
6. ______________________________
7. ______________________________
8. ______________________________
9. ______________________________
10. ______________________________

CHAPTER FOUR

STOCK HUNT - FROM HERE AND THERE

""The single most powerful asset we all have is our mind. If it is trained well, it can create enormous wealth in what seems to be an instant." Robert Kiyosaki (Author: Rich Dad Poor Dad)"

"Life isn't about waiting for the storm to pass, it's about learning to dance in the rain." - Vivian Greene (British writer)"

Don't buy stocks on tips and recommendations. You must have heard this now and then. You might also have heard someone losing money if investing based on tips and recommendations.

You know what? The above statement is partially wrong. Tips and recommendations are good to go with.

But wait !!

Don't go with them blindly. Whenever you get any tips or recommendations, do your research. It is not always that tips are wrong. They may be right. They may be so right to build you a fortune. All you need to do is to do the proper research.

Now what are the sources of such tips or recommendations?

Finance Applications

Finance Applications like Money Control App, Xpro India, Indiatimes, Stockedge, and Tickertape keep on providing stock recommendations. Although the recommendations provided by these applications are based on thorough research, you are also required to verify the research. This is the essence of self-learning.

Although free information is available in abundance today, not accepting those pieces of information without self-research is the best way to educate yourself.

So whenever you get any stock recommendations through these apps, no matter how trustworthy the application is, do your further analysis before investing because it is your hard-earned money, not theirs. We shall learn about how to do research or due diligence in "The Final Assault" Chapter.

Social Media Groups

These days joining a YouTube Channel, Telegram Channel or Group, WhatsApp group or any other community that provides stock investment tips and recommendations is very common. These may be the potential reason for the loss of wealth of investors.

I have observed that if someone comes to know about a stock, in the majority of cases, the person invests in the stock blindly without doing the required due diligence. Consequently, losses are faced.

So it's not that you have to rely upon or ignore the stock recommendations. These are the ideas or sources to get the stock name. Once you get the names, perform the due diligence or research yourself.

Friends and Peers

We all have friends and peers who are stock market or investment enthusiasts. They keep on talking about their return on investment. More often we also get to know about the companies they invest in. But wait, this was their research. Even if you are influenced by their stock selection, do your due diligence before investing in their portfolio.

Do you know why ?

You might be under the assumption that the person has a well-researched and performing portfolio. But it is not always that the investment was done by the person himself. He also might have relied upon some tips and recommendations.

So the best way is, to pick the stock idea from here and do the research yourself and invest in a portfolio that suits your risk appetite.

News and Articles

While surfing on the internet or while reading a newspaper, especially the business newspaper or the business column, you will come across the names of some high-performing stocks. Now only two things can happen. Either you will ignore it and scroll up or you will search for the stock and invest in it in anticipation that your portfolio will also be in green.

If you are really lucky, it might come true for you as well. But why take that chance? Pick the idea of stock from here and perform your due diligence before such an investment.

Below are few screenshots from different platforms.

Source : https://economictimes.indiatimes.com/

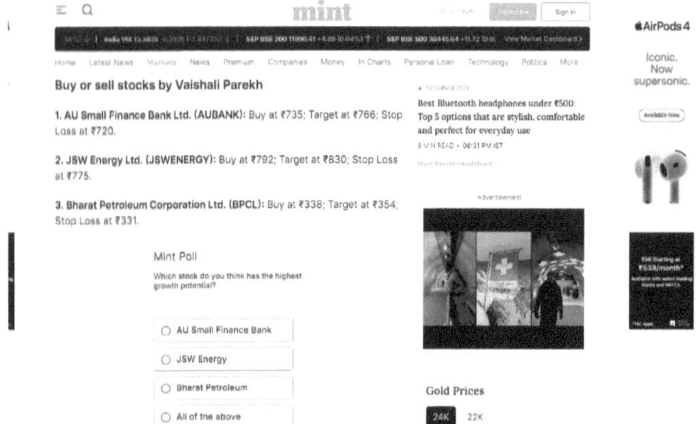

Source : https://www.livemint.com/

The idea is not only restricted to these sources. All you need is to keep your eyes and ears open. You never know from where you can get an idea. It may also come from someone talking in the metro you overheard the stock. Do your research there itself. You have your mobile phone in hand. Why wait for the late?

So, by now you have got an idea of how to pick stocks for your due diligence. Mind it! I am not saying ideas for your portfolio. It's just an idea to find an unknown stock.

I hope you got what I wanted to say in this chapter.

Activity

Find 5 unique stocks from here and there through all 4 channels and list them down. Let's see how much your senses are open

Finance Applications

____

____

____

____

Social Media Groups

____

____

____

____

Friends and Peers

____

____

____

____

News and Articles

____

____

____

____

Stock Hunt - From Screeners

""The stock market is filled with individuals who know the price of everything, but the value of nothing."- Philip Fisher (Economist)"

""Investors should purchase stocks like they purchase groceries, not like they purchase perfume."- Benjamin Graham"

Using a screener is the last resort for me. When observation and here-and-there techniques don't work, I use screeners to hunt a stock for me. Screeners are easy to use. I normally use three screeners.

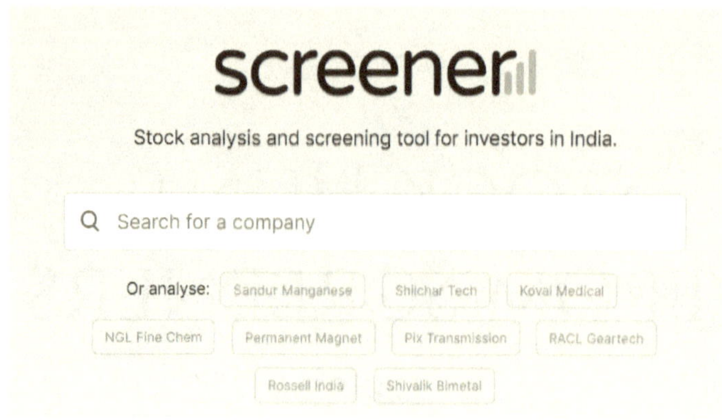

https://www.screener.in/

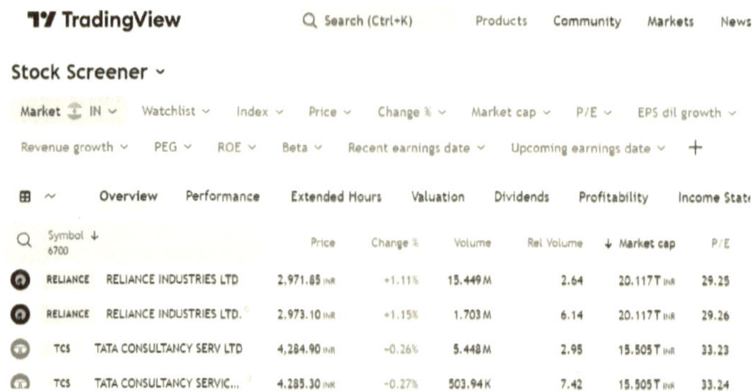

https://in.tradingview.com/screener/

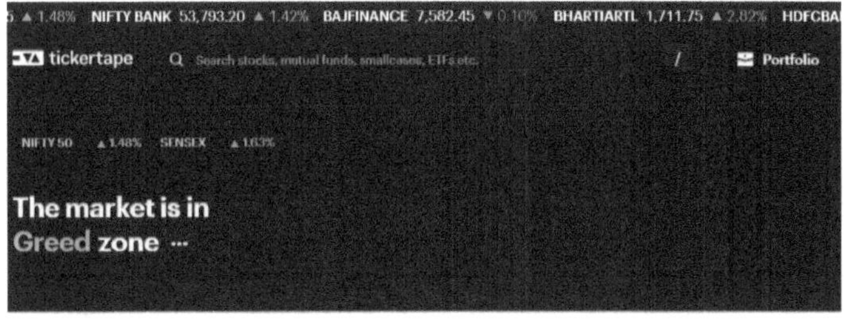

Market and sectors

https://www.tickertape.in/screener/equity

Steps to follow

- In any of the screeners, filter out the companies with market capitalization in ascending order.
- Pull out one report from 0 to 500 crores and another report from 500 crores to 5000 crores separately.
- It would provide a list of micro-cap and small-cap stocks.
- Now using various parameters keep filtering out the stocks. (We shall discuss about the required parameters in the chapter - 'The Final Assault')

And that's it. This was so simple.

Wait !!!

This chapter is not yet over. There is another screener already refined for you. That screener is going to provide you with a list of best of the micro and small-cap stocks.

Can you guess ? Which screener I am talking about ?

Yes, you guessed it correctly. I am talking about the Indices.

Not every stock is eligible to be a part of the Stock Market Index. For a stock to be a part of an Index has to work hard and fulfil some criteria.

- Stock has to meet certain market cap criteria
- Its daily traded volume is considered other criteria
- The average daily delivery volume is another criteria
- Stock performance over past periods is another criteria

Therefore stocks that are part of any Index are more likely quality stocks that can be easily considered for investment, obviously after self-research and due diligence. But yes, picking a stock from an index is not a bad idea to go with.

Below are some indices that can be used for hunting micro-cap and small-cap stocks.

- NIFTY SMALL CAP 100
- NIFTY SMALL CAP 250
- NIFTY MIDSMALL CAP 400
- NIFTY MICROCAP 250
- BSE SMALL CAP
- BSE 400 MIDSMALL CAP
- BSE 250 SMALL CAP
- BSE SMALL CAP SELECT

Here is the link for all these indices

- NSE INDEX - https://www.nseindia.com/market-data/live-market-indices
- BSE INDEX - https://www.bseindia.com/markets.html

So what are you waiting for ? Let's do an activity and find some 10 micro-cap or small-cap stocks from these Indices

Activity

Find 10 unique stocks from a mix of all the NSE indices and 10 unique stocks from a mix of all the BSE indices

NSE Index Stocks

____

____

____

____

____

BSE Index Stocks

____

____

____

____

____

CHAPTER SIX

THE FINAL ASSAULT

""Though tempting, trying to time the market is a loser's game. $10,000 continuously invested in the market over the past 20 years grew to $63,636. If you missed just the best 30 days, your investment was reduced to $11,484.1" - Christopher Davis (American Investor)"

Woah !! Finally, we are here. This is the chapter you must be looking forward to. Please do not expect much from this chapter, because I read somewhere that "***Excess of anything is bad***".

You are not required to learn so many things for a multi-bagger stock hunt. Only a few important things are to be kept in mind. One of them is to find a stock for further analysis. You have already gone through Chapters - 3,4 and 5 where I discussed how to first identify a stock through various techniques.

Let's move on to the Due Diligence part to decide whether the stock should be a part of our portfolio or not.

For this, I have divided this concept into 6 steps as under. I call it the **Hexagon Approach**. Let's discuss.

- Sector Identification
- Competitors List
- Clientele
- Financial Analysis
- Management Outlook
- Institutional or HNI Holdings

Sector Identification

"My investment strategy, which is to focus on sectors that are a national priority for India, hasn't changed.- Gautam Adani (Chairperson of Adani Group)"

*"Invest in good, solid companies in good sectors.
- John Layfield (American commentator)"*

My 10-plus years of experience in this market have taught me so many things worth sharing with my readers. I have come across many investors and traders during this period. When I ask someone randomly about which sector he/she is interested in investing in, I get only 2 answers.

Either the person is biased toward a sector or he hardly cares about any sector. But these days, a third and reasonable answer is coming and that is the one in which I also believe.

Can you guess what?

Yes, you guessed it correctly. I am least bothered about any sector. I am always towards the emerging and trending sector.

So if you ask about my personal choice as a multi-bagger investor. I like to invest only in 2 sectors as of now.

- Green Energy Sector
- Chemical Sector

But my investments are not limited to these two sectors only. Opportunities lie everywhere. It's just that these 2 are my favourites and the majority of the investment is oriented towards these two only.

So before making any investment, identify the sectors you love to invest in and align the majority of your portfolio towards. This will keep your interest in tracking the latest news and developments in the sector and your investment.

Let's get through a few examples from my portfolio, how my sector interest helped me grow my portfolio.

First, I have already discussed about **Olectra Greentech Limited** in my earlier chapter. Although Olectra Greentech is a Bus manufacturing company i.e. it belongs to the Automobile Sector; I selected it because it manufactures battery-operated e-buses which is clearly related to the Green Energy Sector.

It is not necessary to identify a sector exclusively. It may be a combination of two or more like in my case, it was a combination of Green Energy plus Automobile.

The second stock from my portfolio that belonged to the green energy sector was **KPI Green Energy Ltd.** Below is the screenshot of my investment.

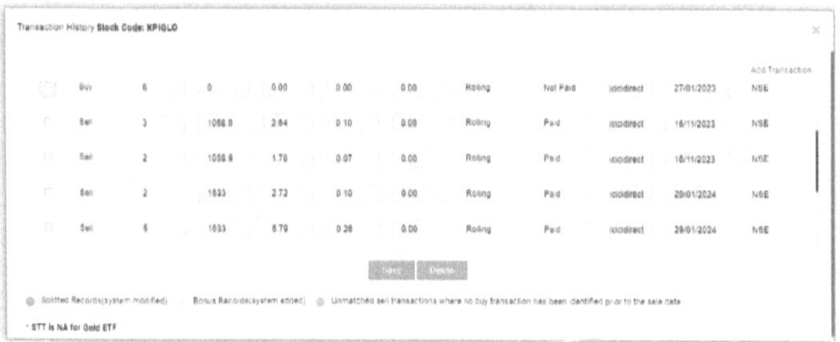

Transaction History **Stock Code: KPIGLO**

Add Transaction

Edit	Action	Quantity	Transaction Price	Brokerage inclusive all taxes	Transaction Charges	StampDuty	Segment	STT Paid / Not Paid	Remarks	Transaction Date (DD/MM/YYYY)	Exchange
	Buy	2	861.25	13.78	0.05	0.00	Rolling	Paid	icicidirect	13/01/2023	NSE
	Buy	4	861.2	27.55	0.10	1.00	Rolling	Paid	icicidirect	13/01/2023	NSE
	Buy	6	0	0.00	0.00	0.00	Rolling	Not Paid	icicidirect	27/01/2023	NSE

Splitted Records(system modified)   Bonus Records(system added)   Unmatched sell transactions where no buy transaction has been identified prior to the sale date

* STT is NA for Gold ETF

Snapshot of KPI Transaction in my portfolio

Transaction History **Stock Code: KPIGLO**

Add Transaction

Edit	Action	Quantity	Transaction Price	Brokerage inclusive all taxes	Transaction Charges	StampDuty	Segment	STT Paid / Not Paid	Remarks	Transaction Date (DD/MM/YYYY)	Exchange
	Buy	6	0	0.00	0.00	0.00	Rolling	Not Paid	icicidirect	27/01/2023	NSE
	Sell	3	1058.0	2.64	0.10	0.00	Rolling	Paid	icicidirect	16/11/2023	NSE
	Sell	2	1058.9	1.76	0.07	0.00	Rolling	Paid	icicidirect	16/11/2023	NSE
	Sell	2	1633	2.72	0.10	0.00	Rolling	Paid	icicidirect	29/01/2024	NSE
	Sell	6	1633	6.79	0.26	0.00	Rolling	Paid	icicidirect	29/01/2024	NSE

Splitted Records(system modified)   Bonus Records(system added)   Unmatched sell transactions where no buy transaction has been identified prior to the sale date

* STT is NA for Gold ETF

Snapshot of KPI Transaction in my portfolio

I first invested in the stock on 13.01.2023 @ Rs 861.25 per share and bought 6 shares of KPI. On 27.01.2023, I received 1:1 bonus share and got 6 shares in my demat thereby raising the count to 12 shares gaining 100% in the very first month. Now my average price per share was Rs 430.63.

Then within 10 months, I sold 5 shares (almost 50% of my holding) @ Rs 1058.90 which was double of my average share price. It means my investment got doubled in just 10 months.

The remaining 7 shares were sold @ Rs 1,633 per share (almost at 4X) within a year. Isn't that great ? If you do the maths correctly, my investment got 3X in just 1 year time. Initial investment in KPI was Rs 5,167.5 and Final take away was Rs 16,725.50.

Let's take the third share from my portfolio. It was **_Suzlon Energy Ltd._** I don't think I need to explain about this stock. But still, I would love to share a glimpse of my portfolio transaction.

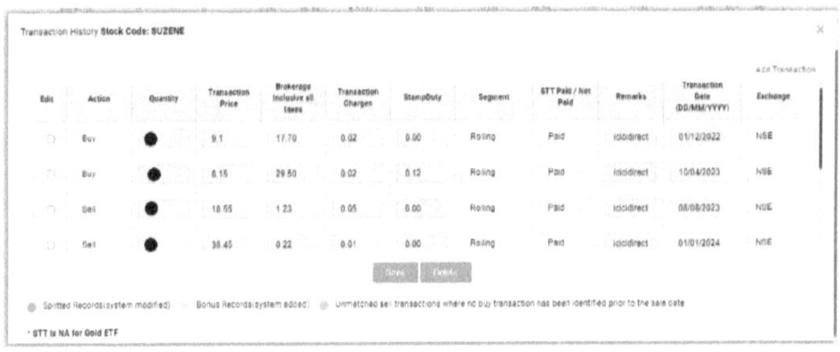

Transaction History **Stock Code: SUZENE**

Edit	Action	Quantity	Transaction Price	Brokerage Inclusive all taxes	Transaction Charges	StampDuty	Segment	STT Paid / Not Paid	Remarks	Transaction Date (DD/MM/YYYY)	Exchange
	Buy	●	9.1	17.70	0.02	0.00	Rolling	Paid	icicidirect	01/12/2022	NSE
	Buy	●	8.15	29.50	0.02	0.12	Rolling	Paid	icicidirect	10/04/2023	NSE
	Sell	●	18.55	1.23	0.05	0.00	Rolling	Paid	icicidirect	08/08/2023	NSE
	Sell	●	38.45	0.22	0.01	0.00	Rolling	Paid	icicidirect	01/01/2024	NSE

Splitted Records(system modified)   Bonus Records(system added)   Unmatched sell transactions where no buy transaction has been identified prior to the sale date

* STT is NA for Gold ETF

Snapshot of Suzlon Transaction in my portfolio

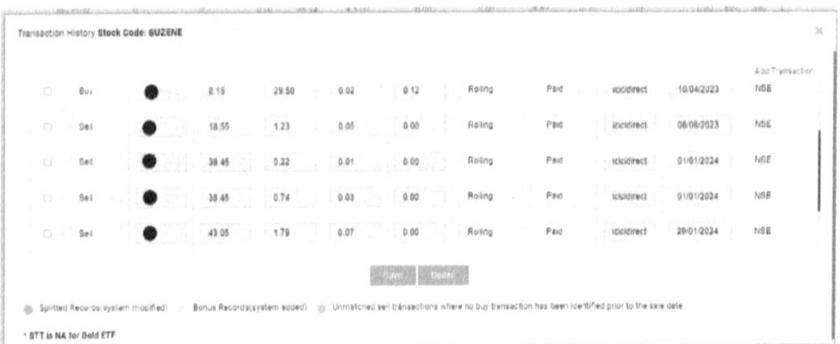

Transaction History **Stock Code: SUZENE**

Edit	Action	Quantity	Transaction Price	Brokerage Inclusive all taxes	Transaction Charges	StampDuty	Segment	STT Paid / Not Paid	Remarks	Transaction Date (DD/MM/YYYY)	Exchange
	Buy	●	8.15	29.50	0.02	0.12	Rolling	Paid	icicidirect	10/04/2023	NSE
	Sell	●	18.55	1.23	0.05	0.00	Rolling	Paid	icicidirect	08/08/2023	NSE
	Sell	●	38.45	0.22	0.01	0.00	Rolling	Paid	icicidirect	01/01/2024	NSE
	Sell	●	38.45	0.74	0.03	0.00	Rolling	Paid	icicidirect	01/01/2024	NSE
	Sell	●	43.05	1.79	0.07	0.00	Rolling	Paid	icicidirect	29/01/2024	NSE

Splitted Records(system modified)   Bonus Records(system added)   Unmatched sell transactions where no buy transaction has been identified prior to the sale date

* STT is NA for Gold ETF

Snapshot of Suzlon Transaction in my portfolio

You can easily observe in my portfolio that my purchases were made in 2 lots @ Rs 9.10 and @ Rs 8.15. I started selling them when it went 2X and the last lot was sold at 5X thereby increasing my investment. This all just happened within 9-10 months.

Another stock related to green energy in my portfolio is *Irm Energy Ltd.* Below is the snapshot.

Transaction History **Stock Code: IRMENE**

Edit	Action	Quantity	Transaction Price	Inclusive all taxes	Transaction Charges	StampDuty	Segment	STT Paid / Not Paid	Remarks	Date (DD/MM/YYYY)	Exchange
	Buy	●	446.9	8.18	0.31	1.47	Rolling	Paid	icicidirect	16/11/2023	NSE
	Sell	●	509.15	0.42	0.02	0.00	Rolling	Paid	icicidirect	29/01/2024	NSE
	Sell	●	509.1	4.23	0.18	0.00	Rolling	Paid	icicidirect	29/01/2024	NSE
	Sell	●	509.1	0.88	0.03	0.00	Rolling	Paid	icicidirect	29/01/2024	NSE

● Splitted Records(system modified)   Bonus Records(system added)   ● Unmatched sell transactions where no buy transaction has been identified prior to the sale date

* STT is NA for Gold ETF

IRM Energy Transaction History

I invested in the stock @ Rs 446.90 on 16.11.2023. But due to some personal requirements, I had to sell it @ Rs 509.15 on 29.01.2024. I reaped a profit of 15% on this. This stock is again a part of my portfolio.

If I discuss about my multi-bagger pick in the Chemical Sector, I would take the name of *Himadri Speciality Chemical Ltd.* Below is the screenshot of my portfolio.

Transaction History **Stock Code: HIMCHE**

Add Transaction

Edit	Action	Quantity	Transaction Price	Brokerage inclusive all taxes	Transaction Charges	StampDuty	Segment	STT Paid / Not Paid	Remarks	Transaction Date (DD/MM/YYYY)	Exchange
☐	Buy	●	100.5	4.45	0.01	0.00	Rolling	Paid	icicidirect	13/12/2022	NSE
☐	Sell	●	382.35	1.59	0.06	0.00	Rolling	Paid	icicidirect	07/02/2024	NSE

Save   Delete

● Splitted Records(system modified)   Bonus Records(system added)   ● Unmatched sell transactions where no buy transaction has been identified prior to the sale date

* STT is NA for Gold ETF

Himadri Speciality Transaction History

As you can see, I bought the shares @ Rs 100.5 on 13.12.2022 and sold them all @ Rs 382.35 on 07.02.2024. It took just 14 months for my investment to become 3.8X. Had I not sold my investment till now, it would have been Rs 641.45 (almost 6.5X in 21 months). This investment also proved to be a multi-bagger for me.

"*Key Takeaway*

A trending or emerging sector can do wonders for your portfolio. But this is not the only criterion. The stock needs to be analysed on the remaining 5 parameters which are discussed in the further sections."

Activity

Identify the sector you want to invest in. Note down the sector and find at least 5 potential stocks for investment. Also, remember that these stocks should be from the stocks identified by you in Chapters 3,4 or 5.

Competitors List

""Companies that solely focus on competition will die. Those that focus on value creation will thrive." – Edward de Bono (Maltese physician)"

Have you ever thought, why stocks of **Titan Company Ltd** proved to be multi-bagger ? Is it just because of brand value ? Or, also because it had very less competitors when it started ?

Competitors here do not mean those small jewellery shops having only 1 or 2 stores. It means listed entities with pan India presence because Titan Company was also at that level. So for an apple-to-apple comparison, you cannot compare a Titan Showroom with a local shop/showroom. As for today, we have PC Jewellers, Kalyan Jewellers, Senco Jewellers etc as the competitors of Titan Company Limited. At the time when Titan was formed in 1984, there was hardly any brand of jewellery that could compete with Titan Company.

So due to low competitors or I should say no competition in the 1980s for Titan, it had gained a huge customer base and the company started growing like anything. And finally, it became a multi-bagger today. The Titan Company Limited has always been the favourite stock of the Bull King Late Mr Rakesh Jhunjhunwala.

Similar was the case with Infosys, Reliance and Wipro in the year 1980s. Due to shallow competition, the shares of these companies have also given a multi-bagger return over the years.

So what's the idea ?

The idea is that with a new emerging sector in the economy, the emerging companies do not have much competition. Slowly when the market grows, competition increases. So, you have to enter these sectors for multi-bagger investment in the initial phase only i.e. when the competition is extremely low.

In my portfolio - I entered **Zomato Ltd** and I am sure many of you would also have subscribed for its IPO. And that's good. Online food delivery is a new edge food tech sector. And of course, Zomato is a market leader in this sector today. So, why not do some research and invest?

Similarly, the Green Energy sector is also an emerging one and I have already discussed my investment in that.

But you know one thing !!

Emerging sectors are not only the ones where competition could be less. Think of those businesses that involve massive capital investment. Can you think of any ?

Let me help you. You can think of those sectors where the situation is monopolistic or government regulatory requirements is very high. For example

- Indian Railways
- Aviation Sector
- Shipping and Logistics Sector
- Port Operations
- Telecom Licence-based sector
- and likewise

Now let me share some of my portfolio investments for your reference. One of the companies that I entered into was **Mazagon Dock Shipbuilders Ltd.** Below is the screenshot for your reference.

Edit	Action	Quantity	Transaction Price	Brokerage Inclusive all taxes	Transaction Charges	StampDuty	Segment	STT Paid / Not Paid	Remarks	Date (DD/MM/YYYY)	Exchange
	Buy	●	214.95	1.90	0.01	0.00	Rolling	Paid	icicidirect	18/02/2021	NSE
	Buy	●	284	35.21	0.11	0.68	Rolling	Paid	icicidirect	03/01/2022	NSE
	Sell	●	307.6	27.24	0.09	0.00	Rolling	Paid	icicidirect	11/08/2022	NSE
	Sell	●	399.35	14.14	0.04	0.00	Rolling	Paid	icicidirect	30/08/2022	NSE

Mazagon Dock Shipbuilders Ltd transactions

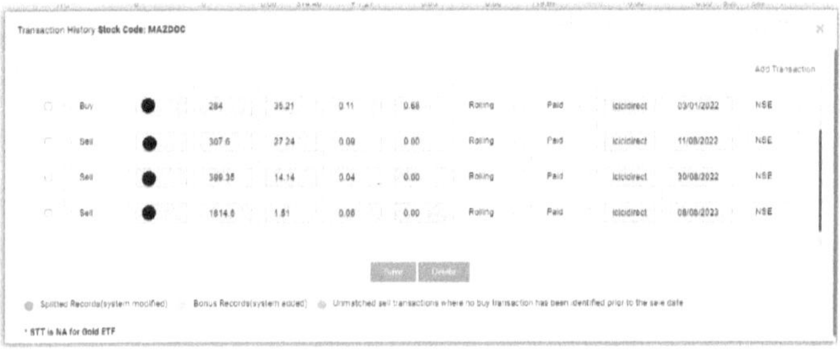

Edit	Action	Quantity	Transaction Price	Brokerage Inclusive all taxes	Transaction Charges	StampDuty	Segment	STT Paid / Not Paid	Remarks	Date (DD/MM/YYYY)	Exchange
	Buy	●	284	35.21	0.11	0.68	Rolling	Paid	icicidirect	03/01/2022	NSE
	Sell	●	307.6	27.24	0.09	0.00	Rolling	Paid	icicidirect	11/08/2022	NSE
	Sell	●	399.35	14.14	0.04	0.00	Rolling	Paid	icicidirect	30/08/2022	NSE
	Sell	●	1814.6	1.81	0.06	0.00	Rolling	Paid	icicidirect	08/08/2023	NSE

Mazagon Dock Shipbuilders Ltd transactions

As you can see I started investing @ Rs 214.95 on 18.02.2021 and sold the final lot @ Rs 1814.60 on 08.08.2023. The investment turned 9X in 2.5 years and if you look at its current price Mazagon Dock is trading @ Rs 4,360.90 (as of 22.09.2024). Had I stayed invested, my investment would have turned 20X in 3.5 years.

Now the question is why I selected this and how I found this. So the answer lies in the first point of the Hexagon i.e. Sector Identification. I started looking for the sectors where the situation is more or less monopolistic and it is not easy for more companies to enter the market.

After a brainstorming thought process, I thought of trying the Ship Manufacturers, which is not an easy market to step into. I came across **Mazagon Dock Shipbuilders Ltd.** I performed my due diligence and finally invested and reaped the results.

Another pick for my portfolio based on Sector Identification and Low Competition was the **Indian Railway Finance Corporation Ltd.** I am sure many of you would have also invested or traded in this stock. Let me share my portfolio with you.

Transaction History Stock Code: INDR

Edit	Action	Quantity	Transaction Price	Brokerage Inclusive all taxes	Transaction Charges	StampDuty	Segment	STT Paid / Not Paid	Remarks	Transaction Date (DD/MM/YYYY)	Exchange
	Buy	●	24.0	1.10	0.00	0.00	Rolling	Paid	icicidirect	01/03/2021	NSE
	Buy	●	21.25	3.76	0.01	0.00	Rolling	Paid	icicidirect	27/04/2021	NSE
	Buy	●	21.25	4.71	0.03	0.00	Rolling	Paid	icicidirect	29/04/2021	NSE

◉ Splitted Records(system modified)   Bonus Records(system added)   ◉ Unmatched sell transactions where no buy transaction has been identified prior to the sale date

* STT is NA for Gold ETF

IRFC Transactions

Transaction History Stock Code: INDR

Edit	Action	Quantity	Transaction Price	Brokerage Inclusive all taxes	Transaction Charges	StampDuty	Segment	STT Paid / Not Paid	Remarks	Transaction Date (DD/MM/YYYY)	Exchange
	Buy	●	31.35	2.50	0.01	0.00	Rolling	Paid	icicidirect	25/11/2022	NSE
	Buy	●	29.75	2.63	0.01	0.00	Rolling	Paid	icicidirect	08/02/2023	NSE
	Sell	●	171.1	2.85	0.11	0.00	Rolling	Paid	icicidirect	29/01/2024	NSE

◉ Splitted Records(system modified)   Bonus Records(system added)   ◉ Unmatched sell transactions where no buy transaction has been identified prior to the sale date

* STT is NA for Gold ETF

IRFC Transactions

My buying price started @ Rs 24.80 on 01.03.2021 and sold my portfolio @ Rs 171.10 on 29.01.2024. It is approximately 7X in 3 years. I know you would also have made some investment and profit in this stock as it was a trending stock at that time. But there must be some difference in the thought process. My selection was based on the concept that this stock belongs to Railway Sector which is not easy for any other company to enter into without government permission. Hence it has a monopolistic environment for growth.

"*Key Takeaway*

Finding a stock that has low competition would be the best selection. And if the sector is emerging, nothing else is better than that. But yes, due diligence has to be done for every stock that you select for your portfolio."

Activity

Identify and list down 5 Stocks that are micro-cap or small-cap and belong to an emerging sector or a monopolistic or duopolistic sector with the lowest competition. Please avoid the shares already discussed in this book.

Clientele

""There is only one boss-the customer. And he can fire everybody in the company from the chairman on down, simply by spending his money somewhere else." - Sam Walton (Founder of Wal-Mart)"

""Whatever you do, do it well. Do it so well that when people see you do it, they will want to come back and see you do it again, and they will want to bring others and show them how well you do what you do." - Walt Disney (Founder of Disney)"

What would a business do without customers or clients ?

What would a business do without a regular or loyal customer ?

What would a business do without a premium client or a high-ticket client ?

The answer to all the questions is the same. The business can sustain itself but cannot grow enormously. Many listed companies show very low growth in terms of share price appreciation. Although the business may be debt-free, although the business may have lower liability, it does not show the growth that it requires. One of the reasons is its client base.

For a company to become a multi-bagger, it has to increase its clientele. And the clientele should be loyal, long term and returning. Service provider companies like IT sector companies, should have enough work orders in their hands to grow within the next 10 years.

There are situations where investors tend to invest in a company that announces obtaining a heavy work order. But that is not an ideal way to invest based on some news.

If I talk about my investment in *Olectra Greentech Limited,* I visited its media coverage section on the website and searched for total work orders completed, new obtained and work orders in the pipeline. When I was extremely satisfied that it has sufficient work order for growth till the next 10 years at least, I decided to invest. Below is the screenshot for your reference.

https://olectra.com/news-media

Another stock from my portfolio that I have discussed earlier is *KPI Green Energy Ltd.* KPI has a very strong clientele that convinced me to invest in the company. Below is the screen-shot for your reference.

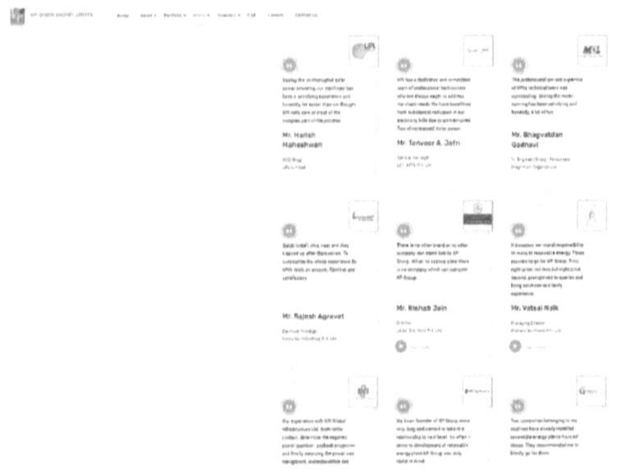

https://www.kpigreenenergy.com/clients-testimonials.html#client

Another multi-bagger from my portfolio which I have not discussed till now is **_GARDEN REACH SHIPBUILDERS & ENGINEERS LIMITED._** If you measure this stock on the first point i.e. Sector, it belongs to the ship manufacturing and repairing sector which requires several government approvals. If you measure it on the second point i.e. competitor list, it belongs to a sector where competition is very low or you can say monopolistic.

Now if you measure it on the third point i.e. Clientele, it has a very strong clientele as it primarily engaged in ship-building activities for the Indian Navy and the Indian Coast Guards. So you can easily understand that this company will always have a demand as it serves for National Security. Also, it is not easy for any other company to enter this sector and hence it can be called a kind of monopolistic situation.

https://www.grse.in/

Below is the screenshot of my investment in *GARDEN REACH SHIPBUILDERS & ENGINEERS LIMITED.* Let's have a look.

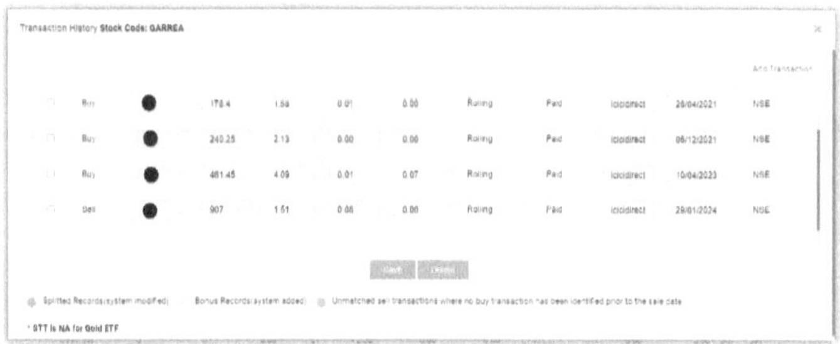

Garden Reach Transactions

As you can see I started buying the shares @ Rs 178.4 on 26.04.2021 and sold them all @ Rs 907 on 29.01.2024. My investment turned approx 3X in 2.5 years. Had I not sold the shares, my portfolio would have been @ Rs 1,848 per share (as of 22.09.2024).

> *"Key Takeaway*
>
> *A strong client base or customer base is very important for including a stock in a multi-bagger portfolio. But yes, along with this other 5 points are also important to look for."*

Activity

Find and list 10 stocks out of the stocks that you have identified till now that have a very strong customer base. Obviously, the stock should be a micro-cap or a small-cap.

Financial Analysis

"Financial freedom is available to those who learn about it and work for it. - Robert Kiyosaki"

""Never invest in a company without understanding its finances. The biggest losses in stocks come from companies with poor balance sheets." Peter Lynch"

""Make sure you have financial intelligence... I don't care if you have money or you don't have money... you need to go and study finance no matter what." – Daymond John (American businessman and investor)"

Now this is the core of all. Till now whatever you have studied in this book and whatever you are going to study next was qualitative analysis of stock. Now the time has come to get into some quantitative and technical concepts.

This is of extreme importance because if this fails entire portfolio is at stake. While writing this book, I assume all my readers are not finance experts. Hence I do not want you all to engage in complex activities like reading the Financial Statements and doing the calculations for yourself. Several applications and websites will do the job for you. All you need is to know the key parameters you need to look into. So Let's learn *Ratio Analysis.*

Only 5 ratios you have to look at. I normally use Screener or Stock Edge to check the ratios. These are nothing new. Most of you have heard of the ratios that I am going to discuss. The only difference you will find is the way you have to look at these ratios.

1. *Cashflow per share*

This has to be positive. A company with negative cash flow per share can never sustain in the long run. However, this is not always correct for a capital-intensive company like Ship Manufacturing, Aircraft Manufacturing, Electricity or Power Generation Companies, Infrastructure Development Companies etc. Can you guess why this is so ? Let me explain.

Cash Flow has three components - Cash Flow from Operating Activities, Cash Flow from Financing Activities and Cash Flow from Investing Activities. Cash Flow from Investing activities will be negative if the company is investing in increasing its infrastructure or manufacturing units or likewise. And if this is the reason for the heavy cash outflow, it is not bad for the company. Instead, the company may reap amazing results in years to come when the actual production commences.

So whenever you see a negative cash flow per share, don't reject the share directly. Dig a little bit to know the reason of negative cash flow. If the reason is progressive, it may be a green flag. Below is a screenshot that justifies the above statement. Although the cash flow is negative, the share turned out to be a multi-bagger. It's **Garden Reach Shipbuilders and Engineers Ltd.**

Garden Reach Shipbuilders & Engineers Ltd. NSE ▾ GRSE

1,855.60 +154.65 (▲9.1%) 20 Sep 2024, 03:44:10 pm

Prices Deliveries Updates Edge Report Technicals **Fundamental** Financials Shareholding MF Holding Documents Scans Deals

Overview Results **Ratios** Growth Pattern

Cash Flow Ratios ▾   Standalone

	10 years	2015-03	2016-03	2017-03	2018-03	2019-03	2020-03	2021-03	2022-03	2023-03	2024-03
Cash Flow Per Share (Rs)		86.76	341.59	-154.41	-6.46	-9.75	54.81	44.98	-31.05	126.60	-61.71
Free Cash Flow per Share (Rs)		128.91	458.74	30.66	-2.48	-16.96	51.34	43.64	-23.69	138.55	-42.72
Sales to Cash Flow Ratio		21.45	3.91	-4.82	-18.21	-12.42	2.28	2.21	-4.93	1.77	-5.08

Click on the bars for interactive chart

Source: Stock Edge

2. *Debt Equity Ratio*

The lower the ratio, the better is the company. Normally, a manufacturing company is expected to have a high debt-equity ratio because it uses debt to expand its manufacturing units. Service sector companies should normally have the lowest debt-equity ratio or maybe negligible debt-equity ratio.

But if a manufacturing concern has an almost negligible debt-equity ratio, nothing can be better than that. It indicates that the hard phase of setting up the manufacturing unit or capital investment is over, and it is time to reap the fruits. I would again like to share the screenshot of my multi-bagger pick **Garden Reach Shipbuilders and Engineers Ltd.** Have a look. You will find negligible debt in the company.

Source: Stock Edge. Refer for Debt Equity Ratio and Interest Coverage Ratio

3. Interest Coverage Ratio

Interest Coverage Ratio lets you understand how much a company is earning to meet its interest obligation occurring out of debt. Higher the better. In the image above for Garden Reach Shipbuilders, you can see that the interest coverage ratio is sufficient enough to serve the debt. In the year ended March 2024, the ratio is 30.47 times. It means the company is earning 30.47 times its interest liability, i.e. if the interest liability is Re 1, the company is earning Rs 30.47. Isn't that great ? Does it not make the company solvent enough to invest ? Of course, yes.

4. EPS Growth Ratio

Everyone knows Earnings Per Share. But looking at EPS would be like deciding in Isolation. Hence we should always look at the EPS Growth rate over the years. Business is not a perfect thing, but yes it's a wonderful thing. Business can make you a fortune if properly handled.

However, the earnings are not always in the growth phase. Earnings may be up or down and that is completely fine. If a business couldn't achieve even the last year's earnings, it's ok. What is important is at least it should show a positive growth in 6-7 years/quarters out of the last 10 years/ quarters. Let's understand with the help the EPS growth rate of Garden Reach Shipbuilders and Engineers Ltd.

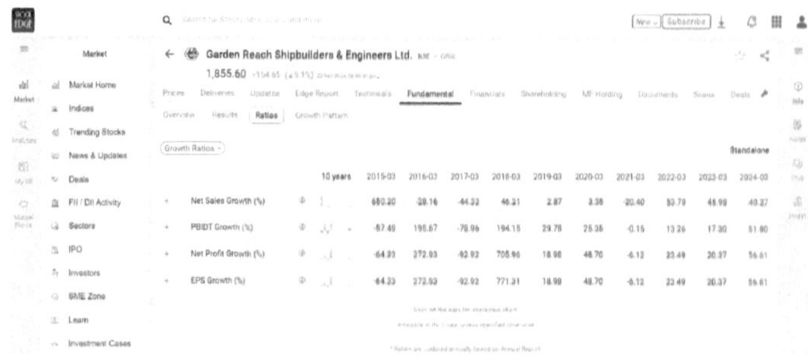

Source: Stock Edge

In the image above, you can see the EPS Growth (%) of Garden Reach Shipbuilders & Engineering Ltd. Out of the past 10 years, EPS has had a positive growth rate in 7 years. This means the company was able to achieve higher income in the current year as compared to preceding years 70% of the time.

5. Return on Equity (ROE)

I do not consider Return on Capital Employed (ROCE) for analysing a stock for a multi-bagger portfolio. ROCE is a comparison of EBIT (Earnings before Interest and Tax) against Total Capital Employed. What if, after payment of interest and tax, the earnings or profit turns out to be negative ?

Anyways, I have to look for the ROE where we compare Net Profit against the Networth. So the last ratio that I consider is ROE which gives me the final picture of the company's growth in terms of profit. As an illustration I have considered the stock of **Tata Steel Limited** for your reference. Below is the image.

	10 years	2015-03	2016-03	2017-03	2018-03	2019-03	2020-03	2021-03	2022-03	2023-03	2024-03
Return on Equity (%)		-11.29	5.96	-0.87	38.95	14.70	1.70	11.33	44.72	7.48	-5.09
Return on Capital Employed (%)		2.92	5.90	6.29	19.57	14.58	3.44	12.44	33.05	13.53	3.61
PBIT		3,460	6,954	7,546	26,411	23,566	6,200	21,450	55,689	34,534	6,361
Capital Employed		1,13,300	1,28,930	1,22,396	1,53,061	1,71,865	1,86,837	1,73,042	1,92,025	1,89,101	1,70,909
Return on Assets (%)		-2.39	1.22	-0.17	9.22	4.16	0.49	3.32	15.86	2.84	-1.77

Image for ROCE

	10 years	2015-03	2016-03	2017-03	2018-03	2019-03	2020-03	2021-03	2022-03	2023-03	2024-03
Return on Equity (%)		-11.29	5.96	-0.87	38.95	14.70	1.70	11.33	44.72	7.48	-5.09
Net Profit		-3,956	2,043	-304	17,564	9,187	1,172	8,190	41,749	8,075	-4,910
Net Worth		31,531	41,458	35,544	58,596	66,650	71,301	73,464	1,14,443	1,03,082	92,036
Return on Capital Employed (%)		2.92	5.90	6.29	19.57	14.58	3.44	12.44	33.05	13.53	3.61
Return on Assets (%)		-2.39	1.22	-0.17	9.22	4.16	0.49	3.32	15.86	2.84	-1.77

Image for ROE

As you can see in the first image, for the year ended 2024, the ROCE is 3.61 which is a positive value. But if you look at the second image, the ROE is -5.09 which is a negative value.

You would have understood the reason by now. The Earnings made by the company were not sufficient enough to meet its interest and tax expense and hence a negative ROE. So, I consider only ROE and not ROCE. Now it's up to you, what you want to consider.

"Important Note:

Most of you would wonder, why I didn't consider the Price Earning (PE) Ratio. Normally the saying goes like this - "If the PE ratio of a company is below its industry PE ratio, it is good to buy the stock of such company because it is underpriced; and if the PE ratio of a company is above its industry PE ratio, it is overpriced and hence it should be avoided"

But for me, the PE ratio doesn't matter. It is not always correct that what we study always fits practically. It means a company with high PE doesn't need to be a bad choice. And why so ?

It's because every company belonging to a particular industry may not belong to that industry entirely. Analysts have their own idea of classifying an Industry. But if you can understand the vision or the essence of the company, you can easily analyse whether to rely on the PE Ratio or not.

Let me explain with an example from my portfolio. I have discussed above my holdings in **Olectra Greentech Ltd.** *Olectra manufactures* buses and is considered a part of the Automobile Industry. But I consider it from the Green Energy Industry.

Why ? It's just because Olectra was not formed to manufacture normal buses. It manufactures e-Buses which is the future. Hence, despite being considered as a company from the Automobile Industry, I look at it as a company from the Green Energy Industry.

So, although it has a very high PE Ratio as compared to its Industry PE Ratio, it is a part of my multi-bagger portfolio. Refer to the PE Ratio Screenshot below. "

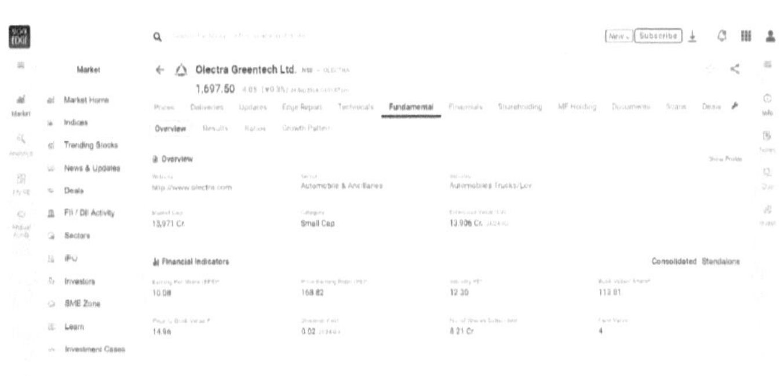

Olectra PE (168.82) v/s Industry PE (12.3)

"Key Takeaway

Not all the ratios are important. As a beginner and learner of multi-bagger portfolio investment, a few important ratios as discussed above can be considered and with experience, other ratios can *also be looked into. Also, never try to pick any stock based on a single ratio. Always analyse at least the 5 ratios discussed above and if required, the PE Ratio."*

Activity

Whatever stocks you have identified till now, write down the 5 ratios discussed above for those stocks along with the PE ratio and find the best pick for you.

Management Outlook

"Ideas are a dime a dozen. It's the execution that's really the important thing and you need really good people for that. Good people can change directions, but there are very, very few truly great people who can execute properly. - Arthur Rock (American businessman and investor)"

"When you find a really good business run by first-class people, chances are a price that looks high isn't high. The combination is rare enough, it's worth a pretty good price. - Warren Buffett"

Understanding the leaders of the business is very important. Even if everything is best, a wrong leader will take no time to put the entire business at stake. And this has happened so many times in past. We have numerous examples of wrong management from history where a flourishing business is put to earth. Few I have mentioned below, few more you can think of.

- Jet Airways (India) Ltd
- Kingfisher Airlines Ltd
- Reliance Communications Ltd
- Alps Motor Finance Limited
- Gujarat NRE Coke Ltd

Do I look at the management ? Of course, I do. So what actually is required to be looked for ? Let me explain.

- Future planning of the management that can be read from the Director's report. But you don't have to just read. You have to see whether they have actually worked according to what they mentioned in the report. It means you are required to look at previous years' Director's report and compare that with the actual performance of the management in the current year. Hence you will be in a position to know whether the management has kept its promise on growth or not.

- Any change in the management, especially the Key Managerial Persons like CEO and CFO. A resignation of a Key Managerial Personnel (KMP) can be a price-sensitive event and may affect a listed company's stock price. The Securities and Exchange Board of India (SEBI) requires listed companies to disclose KMP resignations to stock exchanges within seven days of the resignation's effective date.

- Back in 2022 when Ravi Kumar S, President and KMP of Infosys resigned, the share price saw a negative impact. However since Infosys is a fundamentally strong company with strong leadership under Mr N. R. Narayana Murthy, it regained its loss. Below is a screenshot from ICICI Direct Research on this event.

Source : ICICI Direct

"**Key Takeaway**

Having visionary management is a must for the growth of a company. So never forget to have a look at the management's portfolio. No matter how strong the fundamentals of the stock are, going through the portfolio of management and their vision is mandatory."

Activity

Find and list at least 5 companies that are micro-cap or small-cap where a recent change in management has taken place and the impact on it's share price is negative.

____

____

____

____

____

Institutional or HNI Holdings

""The stock market is a device for transferring money from the impatient to the patient." – Warren Buffett."

""It's not how much money you make, but how much money you keep, how hard it works for you, and how many generations you keep it for." — Robert Kiyosaki"

After you have done all the research and due diligence, you must have identified at least one sure-shot stock for your multi-bagger portfolio.

But wait !! Are you not scared that if anything goes wrong your money will be at stake? This is natural because micro-cap or small-cap stocks are highly risky and all the care should be taken before putting in your hard-earned money.

So how to vouch, whether your hand-picked stock is a multi-bagger or not? Or, even if not a multi-bagger, it is worth investing ?

Well ! I have a way for you. And that's simple. All you need is to look for HNIs Portfolio or Institutional Portfolio.

What ? How can we do that ?

I will tell you that later. First, let's understand why and how should you do that.

You as an individual investor can at best find a stock for you. But if you are a beginner in creating a multi-bagger portfolio for yourself, trust me you will think 1000 times before investing, even if you have done the due diligence thoroughly.

So below are the few steps that you can use to vouch whether your pick is a good choice or not.

- Whenever you find a stock, please look for it in some mutual funds portfolio of small-cap or micro-cap funds. Institutional investors do a hell lot of research before investing even a single penny. Just go for it. If you find your identified stock as a part of any mutual funds portfolio, it's a green flag for you. Go for it and invest.

- What if you don't find your stock in any of the mutual fund's portfolios? Don't get disheartened. Search for its existence in any HNI portfolio. It sometimes happens that due to SEBI regulation on investment by Mutual Funds, the stock identified by you could not become a part of any fund. No worries, if they are really good, they form part of the HNI Portfolio.

- What if your stock is neither a part of MF Portfolio nor HNI Portfolio ? Should you drop it ? Of course not. After putting in lots of energy and time in the research, dropping a stock is not a better option. Instead, have faith in yourself, and take the risk. Invest only 25% of the amount that you had thought of investing in the stock. This will give you the courage to believe in yourself and enhance your skills.

How do I find out whether a stock is a part of a Mutual Fund's Portfolio or a HNI Portfolio ?

For HNI Portfolio I keep following news and keep making a note of it. That is also a source of information that can provide you with a stock idea.

For Mutual Fund's Portfolio, I use Stock Edge and Value Research. These are the two platforms where you can easily find the existence of any stock in any Mutual Fund Portfolio.

Lloyds Engineering Works Ltd is a share from my portfolio which turned out to be a multi-bagger. Below is the screenshot for your reference.

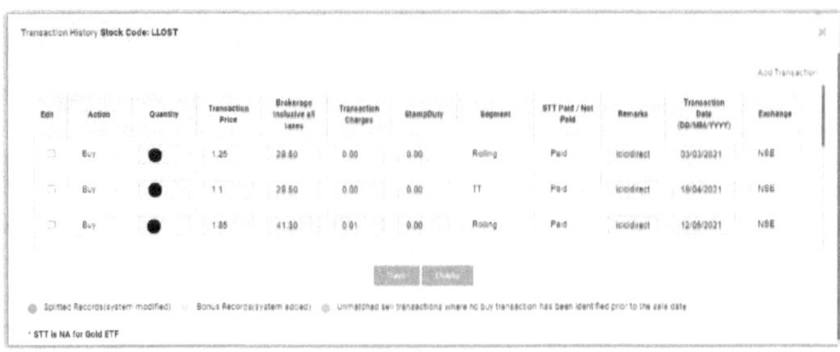

LLoyds Engineering Transaction

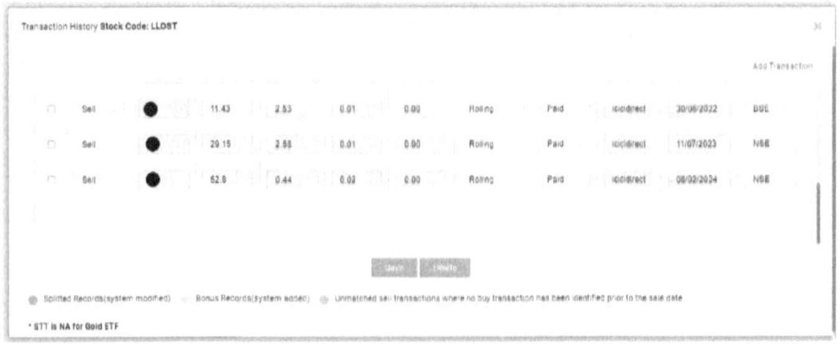

LLoyds Engineering Transaction

As you can see in the portfolio, I started buying the shares @ Rs 1.25 on 03.03.2021 and started selling from Rs

11.43 on 30.06.2023 to Rs 52.8 on 08.02.2024. This turned out to be the greatest multi-bagger of my portfolio as it gave my 11X to 52X return. Had I kept these shares till now, it would have given me a return of 80X. Isn't that amazing ?

Now let's see which Mutual Funds have their holding in this company. For this, I am sharing a screenshot from Stock Edge Website. Please have a look.

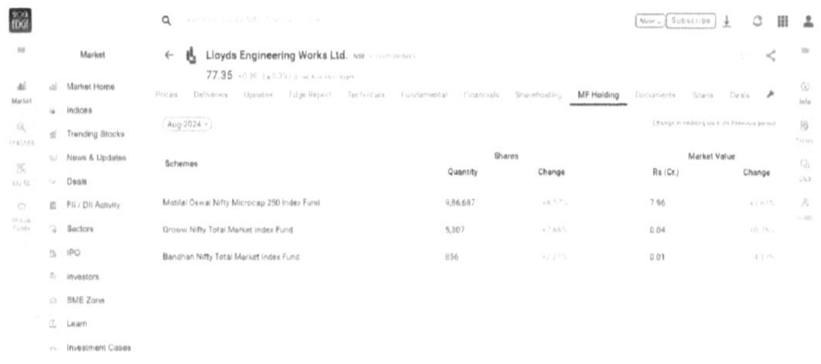

Source : Stock Edge

So you can see from the image that this micro-cap stock is held by 3 mutual funds out of which 1 is a micro-cap fund. This way you can find whether the stock you identified is a part of any Mutual Fund Protfolio. If its yes, go for it.

> **"Key Takeaway**
>
> *If you want to increase your efficiency in multi-bagger portfolio building, you can consider the mutual funds portfolio or HNI portfolio as your guide. And please don't take it otherwise that why to make so much effort. Let's pick stocks from the Mutual Fund Portfolio. It's not like that. Mutual*

Funds have a different playground for their investment. They have a larger pool of money incoming every day. But that's not the situation with you. Your goals are different and resources are limited. So please don't make this mistake."

Activity

Till now whatever stocks you have identified, list all those that are part of the Mutual Funds Portfolio or HNI Portfolio below. Now these are the stocks that could be potential multi-baggers for your portfolio.

CHAPTER SEVEN

PRECAUTION

" "Investing should be more like watching paint dry or watching grass grow. If you want excitement, take $800 and go to Las Vegas." — Paul Samuelson (American economist)"

" "You get recessions, you have stock market declines. If you don't understand that's going to happen, then you're not ready, you won't do well in the markets." — Peter Lynch"

The Thumb Rule

"Do not sell your investment unless you need to do it badly."

Do not stop learning about the company in which you have invested for the long term. It should not happen that you forget your investment and don't exit when you were supposed to. Sometimes it happens that in the urge for long-term investment, people invest and stop tracking the company's performance periodically. And when they look back after a significant period, the company has witnessed a downfall. For example in the case of Jet Airways, Reliance

Communication etc.

You should maintain a habit of tracking all the news and events related to the company in which you have invested. This will allow you to exit from your investment in stressful situations for the company. In case you can't do this monitoring due to any reason, please don't invest in small-cap or micro-cap stocks. Instead, go for Mutual Funds Investment and stay in peace.

Thank You Readers !!

*" "This idea of selfishness as a virtue, as opposed
to generosity: That, to me, is unnatural."*
- Jessica Lange (American Actress)"

First of all, thank you so much for buying this book and showing your trust and love. I am grateful that you considered me to be a part of your learning journey. Writing can often feel like a lonely affair—hours and days spent in front of a blank page, wrestling with ideas and emotions. Yet, knowing that my words might help you build your fortune or if not fortune, your first step towards multi-bagger or value investing has been a constant motivation.

Each time I hear from you - through online reviews, connections or talks, I will be reminded of the great community that is on and around this book, the community that chose me to be a part of its investment journey.

I would love to thank you again for believing in my ideas, thoughts and process of building a multi-bagger stock portfolio. I hope I didn't disappoint you through your learning journey in this book. After the successful writing of this first book of mine, I am tempted to write a few more books that could help you learn more about your investment journey.

Hope you will enjoy those too !

Thank you all once again. With lots of love and wishes for your investment journey.

Signing off
CA Bhaskar Abhishek

THANK YOU READERS !!

THANK YOU READERS !!

Reader's Notes

""The discipline of writing something down is the first step toward making it happen." ~ Lee Iacocca (Former president of Ford)"

Please utilize this space to make your notes and do your research !!

www.ingramcontent.com/pod-product-compliance
Lightning Source LLC
Chambersburg PA
CBHW031318130726
47988CB00007B/2876